THE RACIAL JUSTICE MOVEMENT

"What I'm excited about
is that my child gets to say that his mom,
alongside other fierce Black women,
did everything that she could, and we could,
to make this place better for us."
— Patrisse Cullors —

BY KARA L. LAUGHLIN

Published by The Child's World®
1980 Lookout Drive • Mankato, MN 56003-1705
800-599-READ • www.childsworld.com

PHOTOS

Cover and page 4: Alex Edelman/ZUMA Press/Newscom
Interior: AP Photo: Jacquelyn Martin: 10; AP Photo/Charlie Riedel: 14; AP Photo/
Harold Valentine: 9, 28 (right); AP Photo/Jeff Roberson: 26; AP Photo/John
Minchillo: 12, 31; AP Photo/Julie Fletcher: 6; Brian Cahn/Zuma Press/Newscom:
11; Chris Tuite/ImageSPACE/MediaPunch/IPX via AP Images: 27; DS7/Derrick
Salters/WENN/Newscom: 23; Gabriele Holtermann-Gorden/Sipa/Newscom:
18; Karla Ann Cote/Zuma Press/Newscom: 17; Lawrence Bryant/REUTERS/
Newscom: 22; Loren Elliott/Zuma Press/Newscom: 15; Marion S. Trikosko/
Library of Congress, Prints and Photographs Division: 8; Michael Brochstein/
Sipa via AP Images: 24; Nqobile Mthethwa/Teaching for Change: 19; Olivier
Douliery/Sipa via AP Images: 13, 29; Ollie Millington/Rmv/Zuma Press/Newscom:
25; Richard B. Levine/Newscom: 5; Schomburg Center for Research in Black
Culture, Photographs and Prints Division, The New York Public Library: 7, 28
(left); Stephanie Keith/REUTERS/Newscom: 16; Stephen Zenner/Zuma Press/
Newscom: 21; Underwood Archives/UIG/Universal Images Group/Newscom: 20

LIBRARY OF CONGRESS CATALOGING-IN-PUBLICATION DATA
ISBN 9781503854437 (Reinforced Library Binding)
ISBN 9781503854888 (Portable Document Format)
ISBN 9781503855267 (Online Multi-user eBook)
LCCN: 2021930427

Printed in the United States of America

Cover and page 4 caption:
A woman raises her fist
during the March for
Racial Justice in 2017.

CONTENTS

Chapter One

A BOY IN A HOODIE

On February 26, 2012, a Black seventeen-year-old named
Trayvon Martin was walking down the street in Sanford, Florida.
He was returning from a snack run to the store. It was a chilly
night for Florida, and he was wearing a hooded sweatshirt. In
a nearby truck, George Zimmerman, a white man of Hispanic
descent, watched Martin closely. There had been some burglaries
in the area, and Zimmerman was part of a neighborhood patrol
trying to stop crimes. Zimmerman used his cellphone to call the
police. What happened next led to a violent tragedy that would
capture the attention of the whole country, and even the world.

A mural in Brooklyn,
New York shows
Trayvon Martin in his
hooded sweatshirt.

That tragedy would change the way Americans talked about race. It would force cities and states to look at **racist** patterns in their legal systems and law enforcement programs. It would inspire people from all over the country to come together. They would march and speak and meet with leaders to demand better. Those people are the engine of today's racial justice movement.

Protesters gather in support for Trayvon Martin in 2012.

Chapter Two

AMERICA'S PROBLEM WITH RACE

Black Americans have been denied equality since before the United States became a country. Enslaved Africans were first brought to the United States in 1619. Slavery was common in many states until 1865, when it was outlawed by the Thirteenth **Amendment** to the **Constitution**.

But even when formerly enslaved people gained their freedom, they were not treated as full citizens. **Segregation** was common throughout the United States, especially in the South. After segregation was declared illegal in 1964, white people with power found other ways to keep power from Black Americans. This created a second-class life for most Black people. People of color are still feeling the effects of those racist policies today.

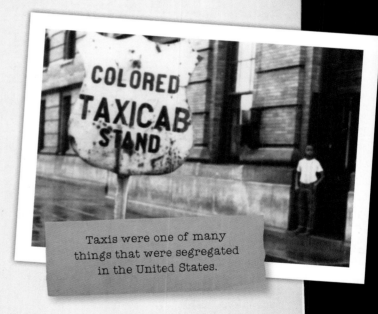

Taxis were one of many things that were segregated in the United States.

Often, the fight for equality has been met with violence. Hate groups like the **Ku Klux Klan** (KKK) formed after the Civil War (1861–1865). Their goal was to ensure that Black Americans never felt safe in their own country. After the First World War, the KKK and other groups of racist citizens started race **riots** and **lynchings** during the Red Summer of 1919. In the 1950s and '60s, Black Americans protesting segregation and Jim Crow laws were again met with violence. Sometimes the victims of this violence were white, but most of the time, the aggressors were white and the victims were Black.

Often the police added to the violence. Police officers, the government, and the legal system often went easy on the white criminals and punished the Black victims of the violence. Each time, Black Americans stood up to demand better treatment.

People view the damage from a bomb at the Birmingham, Alabama home of Black lawyer Arthur Shores.

Chapter Three

STAND YOUR GROUND

Today's racial justice movement builds on the movements of the past. The struggle for racial justice has never ended, and today's racial justice movement is a continuation of that struggle. But just like the **Civil Rights movement** of the '60s, today's racial justice movement is riding a wave of new energy and activity. This wave can be traced back to that encounter between Trayvon Martin and George Zimmerman.

When George Zimmerman called the police about Trayvon Martin, the dispatcher told him not to follow Martin. Zimmerman didn't listen. He followed Martin in his truck. Eventually, according to Zimmerman, the two argued and fought. Trayvon Martin started to win the fight, but George Zimmerman had a gun. He shot and killed Trayvon Martin.

Demonstrators in 1964 march in front of an area formerly used to sell enslaved people in St. Augustine, Florida.

Martin's mother speaking to the press in 2012.

The news of what happened shocked the nation and the world. George Zimmerman claimed Trayvon Martin had attacked him. He said he shot Martin in self-defense. Others said it was a fight that never should have happened and a death that should have been avoided. Florida has a **"Stand your ground" law.** The law says that a person who thinks their life might be in danger is allowed to kill the person that is threatening them. Even if the other person doesn't have a weapon. Even if the shooter could just get away instead.

At first, Zimmerman wasn't arrested for the murder of Trayvon Martin. Police said there was no evidence he had acted illegally. After a public outcry, George Zimmerman was arrested and a trial date was set for 2013.

Zimmerman said he followed Martin because the boy looked "suspicious." Many people, especially people in the Black community, thought Martin looked "suspicious" to Zimmerman simply because he was Black. Suspecting that someone is more likely to commit a crime simply because of their race is called **racial profiling**.

On July 13, 2013, George Zimmerman was found not guilty of killing Trayvon Martin. Many people, especially people in the Black community, were devastated and outraged. Trayvon Martin's parents spoke out, saying racism was what set Zimmerman free. They said racism was what made Zimmerman think Martin was a threat in the first place. They were not alone.

Chapter Four

WE MATTER ...
OUR LIVES MATTER

Black **activist** Alicia Garza says she thought of her brother when Zimmerman was found not guilty. Her brother was young and Black. He also didn't look like most people in his community. He wore clothes like Trayvon wore. If Trayvon could be shot walking home from a snack run, then so could her brother.

Garza wrote on Facebook about the court decision, reflecting on what it means to be Black in America. She ended her post with the phrase, "We matter...Our lives matter." Her friend Patrisse Cullors responded to Garza's post and

Alicia Garza was born in 1981 in Oakland, California.

added #BlackLivesMatter to her response. The hashtag took off on social media. The next day, Patrisse Cullors and Alicia Garza reached out to another friend and activist: Opal Tometi. They decided to start a Black Lives Matter **campaign**.

People of all races
marching behind a Black
Lives Matter banner
in New York City.

When Cullors led a march for racial justice later that week, she
brought a #BlackLivesMatter banner along. On social media, people used
the hashtag to talk about racial justice issues. They also used it to share
their stories of encountering racism. People began holding Black Lives
Matter signs at protests. The Black Lives Matter movement was born.

Chapter Five

"I CAN'T BREATHE!"

The Black Lives Matter campaign became much better known in 2014. On July 17, a Black man named Eric Garner was stopped by police for selling cigarettes illegally in New York City. One of the officers put Garner in an illegal choke hold. Garner told officers "I can't breathe," many times, but he was kept in the choke hold until his body went limp. He died in the hospital later that day. A friend of Garner's used his phone to record a video of the encounter. He gave it to the *New York Daily News*, who published it. The video sparked Black Lives Matter protests in New York City and around the country.

A crowd gathers to march in Washington, DC in 2014.

Not long after that, on August 9, Darren Wilson, a white police officer, shot and killed 18-year-old Michael Brown in Ferguson, Missouri. Witnesses said that Brown had his hands up and was yelling "Don't shoot" when the officer shot him. That night, protesters gathered. After a vigil for Brown, some of the protesters damaged property and looted businesses. Police officers used tear gas and shot rubber bullets at the protesters. They drove armored trucks down the street.

The demonstrations in Ferguson continued for months. People from across the country held protests at home. Black Lives Matter organized a Freedom Ride to Ferguson. People from all over traveled to Ferguson to join the protests and learn to be activists when they returned home.

Police watch protesters as they gather in Ferguson, Missouri on November 25, 2014.

The words "I can't breathe" and "Hands up, don't shoot" became rallying cries for the racial justice movement. In the months and years that followed, the deaths of more Black men and women at the hands of police officers were shared on social media.

November 22, 2014: Tamir Rice.

April 12, 2015: Freddie Gray.

July 6, 2016: Philando Castile.

Many others as well. With each death, people marched in the streets.

The protests in Ferguson and elsewhere inspired other activism. Professional athletes began kneeling during the singing of the National Anthem at games. It was their way of honoring the lives of the people who had died. Symbols of the Civil War, like the Confederate flag and statues of Confederate soldiers, began to be removed from public spaces. Sometimes cities and towns decided to remove them. Sometimes demonstrators removed them on their own.

San Francisco 49ers Eric Reid (35), Colin Kaepernick (7), and Eli Harold (58) kneel during the national anthem before a 2016 game.

A study by the US Crisis Monitor found that 93% of Black Lives Matter protests did not involve any acts of violence.

Not everyone was supportive of the movement. To some, Black Lives Matter sounded like "Only Black Lives Matter." To them, taking a knee during the National Anthem was unpatriotic. They looked at protests and paid more attention to the violence and looting than to what peaceful protesters were saying.

One group of people who grew upset with racial justice protests organized their own rally in Charlottesville, Virginia. They went there to protest the planned removal of a Confederate statue. The Unite the Right rally was held in August of 2017. It was a gathering of **white supremacist** groups similar to the Ku Klux Klan. On the day of the rally, a man drove into a crowd of **counterprotestors**, killing a woman and injuring 19 others.

Just as had happened during the Red Summer and in the 1960s, the cries for equality were met with violence. But the leaders of the racial justice movement were not intimidated. They just kept pushing forward.

White supremacists carry torches at the 2017 Unite the Right rally in Charlottesville, Virginia.

Chapter Six

THE POWER OF SOCIAL MEDIA

Unlike the Red Summer of 1919 or the 1960s, members of today's racial justice movement have a new and powerful tool: the Internet.

Black Lives Matter leaders used social media sites like Twitter and Instagram to keep their message on people's minds. They used social media to plan protests quickly and widely. Something that happened in a small town in the Midwest could be known by the whole country in a matter of moments. They used social media to spread the word

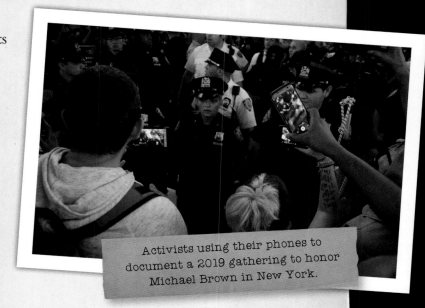

Activists using their phones to document a 2019 gathering to honor Michael Brown in New York.

about other actions, like **boycotts** and letter-writing. And they used it to find one another and gather in their communities to take action.

Students in New York City organize a protest on the steps of the Department of Education building in 2020, demanding racial justice reform and less police presence in their schools

Local Black Lives Matter chapters are as different as their communities. A New York chapter worked with a local school to reduce police involvement with school discipline. An Indiana chapter is working to create fairer housing **policies**. The Washington, DC chapter began a **mutual aid** project that grants money to many different organizations that help people in need.

Educators talk about books at a school fair during the Black Lives Matter Week of Action in Washington, DC.

Chapter Seven

DEFUND THE POLICE?

Why is there so much outcry for change in the policing of America? To understand why, we need to look at the history of police forces in the US.

In the South, the first police forces were volunteer "slave patrols"—groups of three to six men who would search for enslaved people who had escaped. When the southern states adopted their first paid police forces, they often hired people from these slave patrols. Because of this beginning, and a history of police violence in enforcing laws that are unfair to them, many Black people distrust the police.

Martin Luther King Jr. (right) and other marchers are shoved back by Mississippi police during the 1966 March Against Fear.

Some have called for abolishing police forces altogether. They would like to think of new ways for communities to enforce laws and keep people safe. Others just want to limit the jobs that police officers do. They point out that police departments have slowly added responsibilities over the years. They often have to stop family fights that get violent. They are called when homeless and drug-addicted people need help. Some argue that many of the problems that the police handle should be handled by social workers and counselors instead.

Police wear heavy protection as they encounter protesters at a 2020 march in Louisville, Kentucky.

Another change the racial justice movement would like to make is the **demilitarization** of police forces. The US government sometimes sells war equipment to police departments. Many police forces have armored vehicles and military weapons. Critics say these weapons don't belong in police departments. They point out that police officers aren't at war. Their job is to "serve and protect."

People of color have good reason to want changes in police forces. Black people, especially Black men, are more likely to be stopped by police officers than white men. When they are stopped, the interaction is more likely to get physical or end in an arrest. Black people are also more likely to go to prison if they get arrested. This is true even when a Black person and a white person are found guilty of the same crime.

Cori Bush is Missouri's first Black congresswoman. A longtime activist and community organizer, Bush decided to run for office after the death of Michael Brown at the hands of a police officer.

When an organization treats one group of people worse than another because of skin color or ethnic background, it's **systemic racism**. People who don't have racist beliefs can still contribute to

In 2020, Alicia Garza focused on getting people to vote. She told a reporter: "Movements are not just about protests. Movements are absolutely about how we get more power into the hands of more people."

systemic racism. This is because the system (in this case, the police force and the US justice system) has ways of doing things that end up favoring white Americans. Sometimes this happens because people believe white people are better than others. But it can also happen without people realizing they are doing it. When people treat people of other races differently without realizing it, they are showing **unconscious bias**.

One of the goals of the racial justice movement is to eliminate sources of unconscious bias in our culture. Imagine a television show where all of the criminals are Black and all of the crime fighters are white. Your brain is always looking for patterns. That's how we learn. Your brain might decide that white people are safe and Black people are unsafe. You might not even notice that you're starting to think that way. When illustrations in school materials or community centers only show people with light skin, that can send a silent message that only white people are expected there, which could make people of color feel unwelcome.

One way the racial justice movement wants to fight unconscious bias is to encourage **representation** of all types of people in our communities. Organizers are working to help people of color get elected to government positions. They are urging people to pay attention to whether unconscious bias might be keeping people of color out of leadership roles in society.

Marley Dias is a Black teenager from New Jersey. When she was 11, Marley noticed a lack of representation in her school library. She launched #1000BlackGirlBooks to give libraries more books with Black main characters. Her goal was 1000 books, but so far she's collected more than 13,000!

Marley Dias was born in 2005.

Chapter Eight

A TIPPING POINT?

For the first few years of Black Lives Matter, the protesters were mostly people of color. That changed on May 25, 2020, with the death of George Floyd.

George Floyd was a Black man in Minneapolis, Minnesota, who police suspected of using a **counterfeit** $20 bill. During the encounter with Floyd, an officer, Derek Chauvin, pinned Floyd to the ground with his knee on Floyd's neck. He stayed that way for almost nine minutes. Even after Floyd kept saying he couldn't breathe, the officer didn't change position. Bystanders asked officers to check on Floyd, but the police officers nearby did not move. They didn't move until the ambulance

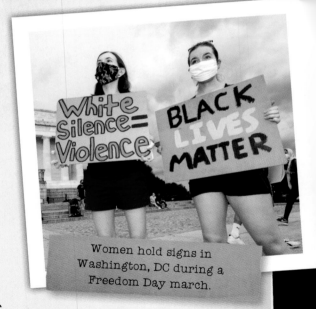

Women hold signs in Washington, DC during a Freedom Day march.

arrived. Floyd died in the hospital shortly after he was taken from the scene.

George Floyd's story reminded many people of Eric Garner. Once again, people staged protests in cities and towns all over the country. But this time, things were different. This time, a lot more of the faces in the crowd were white.

George Floyd's story moved the world. In the month after George Floyd's death, over 4,700 protests were staged in cities and towns in all 50 states and in many countries around the world. Many people hoped that finally the racial justice movement was making progress.

But showing up at a protest is only a part of the work that needs to happen. Change happens when people work at it for months and years. People who don't have to see the effects of injustice every day can easily go back to the old ways of doing things. In June of 2020, 67% of adults in the US said they supported Black Lives Matter. By September 2020, the percentage had fallen to 55%.

A crowd gathers at a park in London, England to protest racism. The gathering was sparked by George Floyd's death.

The racial justice movement is making some progress. The city of Sanford, Florida has new rules for their neighborhood watch: volunteers may not follow people or bring guns on their shifts. All four of the officers involved in George Floyd's death were fired and arrested. Many cities and states banned choke holds after the George Floyd protests. The state of Mississippi removed a Confederate symbol from its state flag. The City of Ferguson hired a Black police chief and more officers of color, including Spanish speakers.

Today's racial justice movement includes people of all races working in many different ways to make life fair for everyone. We have a long way to go to make sure that every American can live in freedom and peace. The quest for racial justice will continue. Every day people pick up signs to protest injustice. They point out places that need better representation. They work to reduce systemic racism. It's hard work, and progress can be slow. But it's important work that any citizen can do. Including you!

Delrish Moss was hired as the first Black chief of police in Ferguson, Missouri.

Protesters raise their
fists during a 2020
march in Washington, DC.

After #BlackLivesMatter became popular, some people started using #AllLivesMatter.
Do you think one saying rules out the other one?
What are the positive outcomes of the slogans Black Lives Matter and All Lives Matter?
What are the negative outcomes?

Trayvon Martin's mother believes he died because of racism.
Do you agree or disagree?
Who was responsible for Trayvon Martin's death?
Could anything have been done to prevent it?

TIME LINE

1600–1799

1619
The first enslaved Africans land in North America at the settlement of Jamestown in what is modern-day Virginia.

1776
The United States declares its independence from Great Britain. Thomas Jefferson writes in the Declaration of Independence that "all men are created equal."

1800

1865
The Thirteenth Amendment to the US Constitution declares slavery to be illegal.

1868
The Fourteenth Amendment declares that any person born within the United States is a citizen.

1870
The Fifteenth Amendment gives Black men the right to vote.

1870s
Jim Crow laws are put into place in the South, enforcing separation of nonwhites from whites.

1950–1970

1950s
Jim Crow laws end in the South with the civil rights movement.

1954
The Supreme Court rules in *Brown v. Board of Education* that the "separate but equal" idea violates the Constitution.

1963
Approximately 250,000 people attend the March on Washington for Jobs and Freedom in Washington, DC.

1964
The Civil Rights Act is passed.

Should police officers have tanks, grenades, and other tools that soldiers have?
What are the benefits?
What are the dangers?

Does representation matter?
Have you ever noticed a place where people like you weren't represented?
Did that affect how you felt about that place?

2010

2012
Trayvon Martin, a Black teen, is shot by George Zimmerman in Florida.

2013
George Zimmerman is found not guilty. In response, activist Alicia Garza uses the phrase "Black lives matter" in a social media post. Activist Patrice Cullors replies, including the #BlackLivesMatter hashtag. The phrase spreads across the country.

2014
Eric Garner, a Black man, dies in July after being put in an illegal choke hold by New York police. Just weeks later, a Black man named Michael Brown is shot and killed by a police officer in Ferguson, Missouri. Protests erupt.

In November, Black teen Tamir Rice is shot by Ohio police while playing with a toy gun which police officers believed was real.

2016
Professional football quarterback Colin Kaepernick protests racial oppression by taking a knee instead of standing for the National Anthem before a game. Other players and athletes from other sports conduct similar forms of protest.

2020

2020
George Floyd, a Black man in Minnesota, is killed after a police officer presses his knee to Floyd's neck for almost 9 minutes. Protests are held across the world to bring attention to racial discrimination and oppression.

activist (AK-tih-vist)
An activist is someone who takes direct action for a particular cause. Alicia Garza is an activist.

amendment (uh-MEND-ment)
An amendment is a change that is made to a law or legal document. The Thirteenth Amendment ended slavery in the United States.

boycotts (BOY-kots)
A boycott is a refusal to buy or use a product or service as a form of protest. The Montgomery Bus Boycott worked to change laws about where people could sit on a bus.

campaign (kam-PAYN)
A campaign is a series of organized actions in order to achieve something. Black Lives Matter is a campaign for freedom and justice for Black people.

Civil Rights movement (SIV-il RITES MOOV-munt)
Civil rights are rights that all citizens should have, no matter what their race or background is. The Civil Rights movement took place mainly in the 1950s and 1960s.

Constitution (kon-stuh-TOO-shun)
The US Constitution is the written document containing the principles by which the United States is governed. The Constitution was amended to outlaw slavery.

counterprotesters (KOWN-tur-PROH-test-urz)
Counterprotestors are people who hold a protest in response to another group's protest.

demilitarization (dee-mil-ih-tayr-iz-AY-shun)
Demilitarization is the doing away with the heavy weapons militaries use. Many activists in the racial justice movement support the demilitarizaion of the police.

Ku Klux Klan (KOO KLUKS KLAN)
The Ku Klux Klan is a group of secret societies opposed to African Americans, Jews, and other minorities. Also called the KKK or the Klan, this white hate group operates in the United States and Canada.

lynchings (LIN-chingz)
A lynching is the taking of a person's life by mob violence, often by hanging. There were lynchings during the Red Summer of 1919.

mutual aid (MYOO-choo-ull AYD)
Mutual aid is a way of sharing group resources to meet the needs of the community. Some mutual aid societies help volunteers find people who need help. Some gather and then give out money.

policies (PAHL-uh-seez)
A policy is a general plan used to make decisions or take actions.

racial profiling (RAY-shul PROH-fyle-ing)
Racial profiling is a habit of treating people of one race as more likely to be criminals.

racist (RAY-sist)
A racist belief is a belief that one race of people is better than another. The United States has long struggled with racist ideas and policies.

riots (RY-uhtz)
Riots are noisy, violent public disorders. There were riots in the Red Summer of 1919.

segregation (seg-ruh-GAY-shuhn)
Segregation is the practice of keeping racial groups apart by maintaining separate schools and public facilities. Segregation was widespread in the United States until it was outlawed in 1964.

systemic racism (siss-TEM-ik RAY-siz-um)
When systems, laws, and processes are set up in a way that puts certain races at a disadvantage, it is called systemic racism. The social justice movement is fighting to end systemic racism.

unconscious bias (un-KON-shuss BYE-uss)
The set of thoughts or beliefs that people have but don't notice. Unconscious bias causes people to make assumptions about others simply based on someone's race, gender, or other group membership.

white supremacist (WITE soo-PREM-uh-sists)
A white supremacist is a person who believes that white people are superior to all other races. The Unite the Right rally in 2017 was a gathering of white supremacist groups.

BOOKS

Alexander, Kwame. *The Undefeated*.
Boston, MA: Houghton Mifflin Harcourt, 2019.

Allen, Tessa. *Sometimes People March*. Fairfax, VA: Library Ideas, 2021.

Celano, Marianne. *Something Happened in Our Town
(A Child's Story About Racial Injustice)*.
Washington, DC: Magination Press, 2018.

Dias, Marley. *Marley Dias Gets It Done: And So Can You!*
New York, NY: Scholastic, 2018.

Elliott, Zetta. *Say Her Name (Poems to Empower)*.
Los Angeles, CA: Disney/Jump at the Sun, 2020.

Ramee, Lisa Moore. *A Good Kind of Trouble*.
New York, NY: Balzer and Bray, 2019.

WEBSITES

Visit our website for links about the Racial Justice Movement:

childsworld.com/links

*Note to Parents, Teachers, and Librarians: We routinely verify our Web links to make sure
they are safe, active sites—so encourage your readers to check them out!*